MW01614324

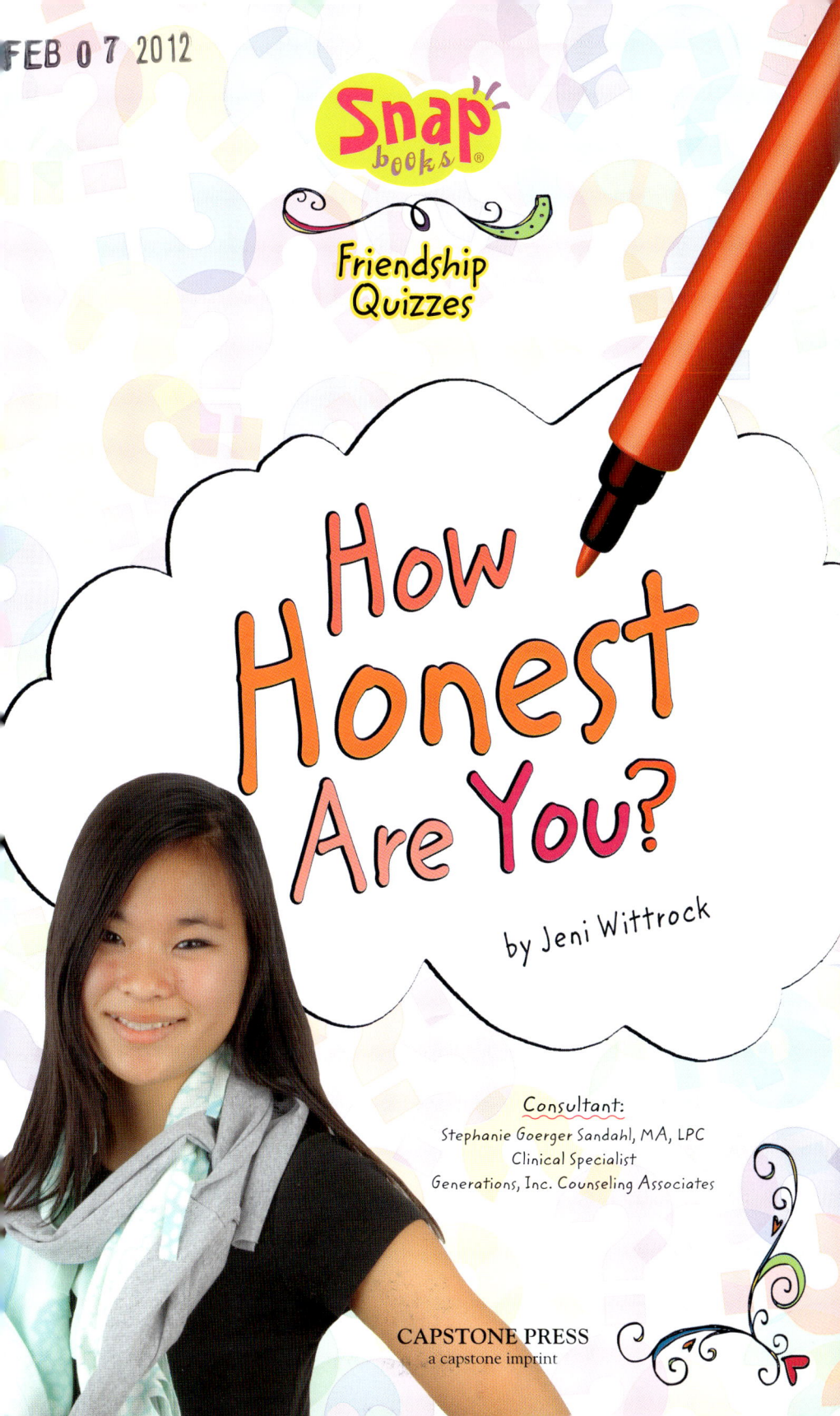

FEB 07 2012

Snap books ®

Friendship Quizzes

How Honest Are You?

by Jeni Wittrock

Consultant:
Stephanie Goerger Sandahl, MA, LPC
Clinical Specialist
Generations, Inc. Counseling Associates

CAPSTONE PRESS
a capstone imprint

Snap Books are published by Capstone Press,
151 Good Counsel Drive, P.O. Box 669, Mankato, Minnesota 56002.
www.capstonepub.com

 Books published by Capstone Press are manufactured with paper
containing at least 10 percent post-consumer waste.

Library of Congress Cataloging-in-Publication Data
Wittrock, Jeni.
  How honest are you? / by Jeni Wittrock.
    p. cm. — (Friendship quizzes)
  Includes index.
  ISBN 978-1-4296-6542-1 (library binding)
  1. Truthfulness and falsehood—Juvenile literature. 2. Honesty—Juvenile
literature. I. Title.

  BF575.T7.J66 2012
  179'.9—dc22   2011001569
  Summary: A quiz about honesty

Editor: Brenda Haugen
Designer: Veronica Correia
Media Researcher: Marcie Spence
Production Specialist: Laura Manthe

Photo Credits: Capstone Studio: Karon Dubke, cover, 1, 4, 9, 15, 18, 26; Shutterstock: absolute-india,
21, Alice, (design element), Ayelet Keshet, (design element), azzzya, (design element), Bevan
Goldswain, 6 (bottom), blue67design, (design element), Brad Sauter, 25, Darrin Henry, 27, Elise
Gravel, (design element), grzhmelek, 16, lineartestpilot, 6 (top), liza1979, 10 (back), Lorelyn Medina,
8, Maaike Boot, (design element), Mastering_Microstock, 13, michaeljung, 23, Monkey Business
Images, 11, 29, naluwan, 19, NLshop, 12 (right), OLJ Studio, 7, Primusoid, (design element), 5,
Thirteen, 12 (left), Tom&Kwikki, (design element), Tracy Whiteside, 22, Traudl, 14, UltraViolet,
(design element), VILevi, 10 (front), zsooofija, (design element)

This book is dedicated to Bethy, Deeter, and Aaron. They definitely aced the
friendship quiz.

Printed in the United States of America in Melrose Park, Illinois.
032011   006112LKF11

Table of Contents

Introduction

Did you ever have a friend who didn't stand behind her promises? A friend who swore she'd never whisper a word of your big secret? And yet, mysteriously, half your grade knew the next week? Yikes! So, why did she act this way? What exactly was your friend lacking? It's called honesty, girls. And it's a big deal.

When you break it down, honesty is simply refusing to be untrue in any way. There is no cheating, no lying, no stealing—no exceptions! It's a rare, outstanding quality in the truest of friends. So, how honest are you? You might think you are honest … most of the time. But what about fibs? Or those harmless little white lies? Do they count? Let's find out just where you fall on the honesty scale, shall we?

Let's be real—one of the best parts of reading magazines is taking the quizzes. After all, who doesn't love learning more about themselves? This book is designed for you to do just that. Take this quiz to discover just how honest you are. From straight-talkin' girls to shifty-tongued tricksters, you'll find all the answers about how truthful you really are.

Even though this is nothing like taking a test at school (it's way cooler!), there are a few things you'll need before you get started. And don't worry—no #2 pencils required.

• Grab a sheet of notebook paper to write your answers down. You'll also need a pen or pencil. Number the sheet from 1 to 15, and you're ready to rock!

AND PLEASE, DO NOT WRITE IN THIS BOOK!!!

• Tell the truth. No one will see your answers but you.

OK ... ready, set, grow!

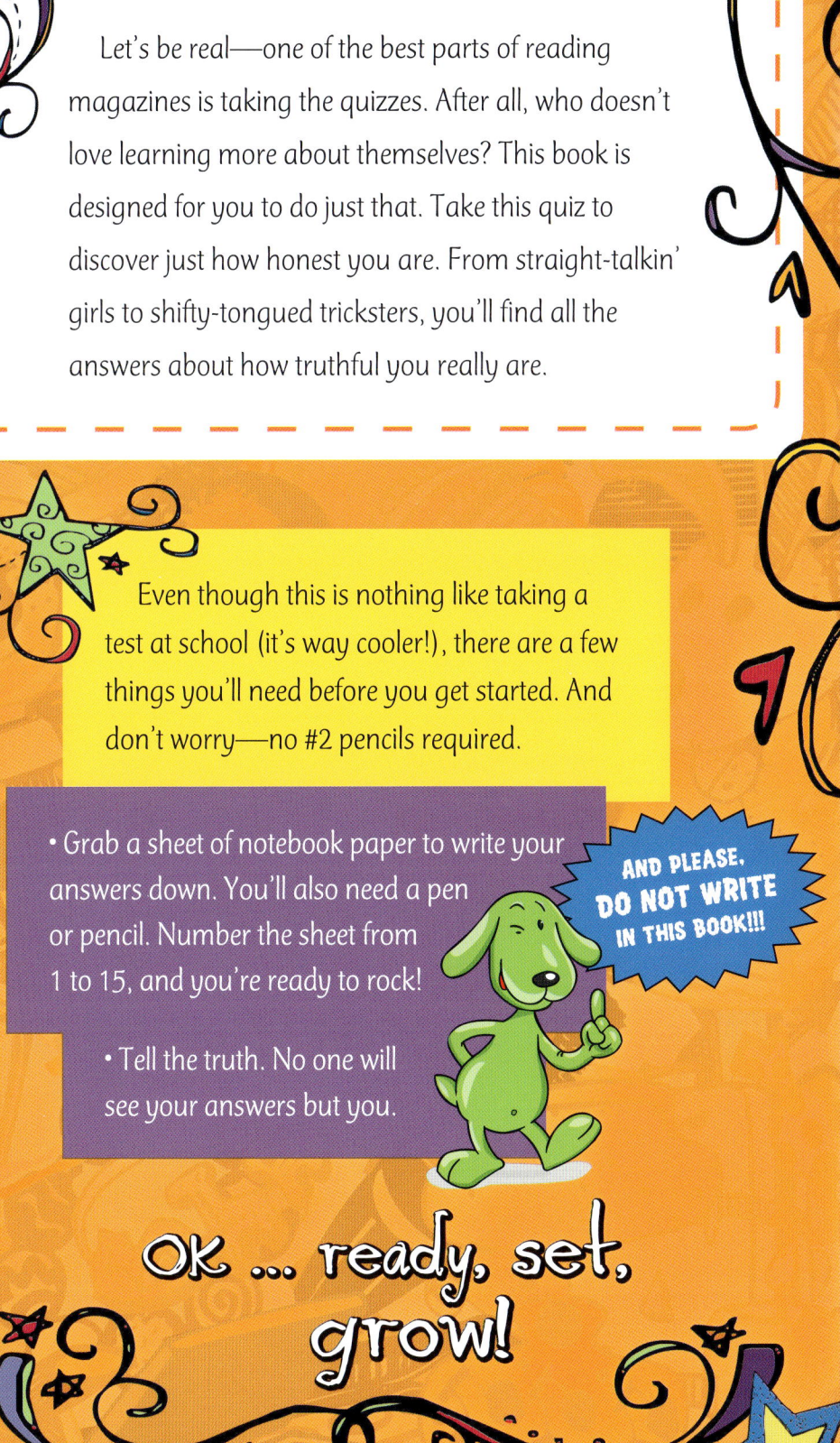

QUIZ

1- Your BFF begs you to go with her to the new vampire flick that opens on Friday. You are SO over the vampire fad, so you:

a) Sigh and say, "Count me in, Miss Dracula."

b) Smile and say, "Thanks, but no thanks! I simply can't stomach another vampire movie."

c) Tell a small lie and say you have to babysit your kid brother Friday night, even though your schedule is totally open.

2- Your algebra teacher asks if you'd tutor some fourth graders who are struggling with math. You are rocking an A in your class, but being a math tutor is not your style. You:

a) Admit that tutoring really isn't your thing, sorry.

b) Slyly cross your fingers and say you'd love to help, but you don't have enough time.

c) Open your planner and say, "Fine. When do we start?"

3- When it comes to scoring deals on clothes, you and your friends are pros. But when a cashier zones out and forgets to scan a pair of leggings, you:

a) Pay for only what he charged you for and walk out of the store feeling lucky. You can't be blamed for his mistake, right?

b) Strike up a lively conversation with him. If you can keep him talking, maybe he won't realize his mistake.

c) Help the guy out and ask, "Did you scan all three leggings? I think you missed the purple pair."

4- A friend invites you to a party at her house Friday night. Her parents are going out, and things could get a little wild. You really want to go, but you know your parents' rule—no parties unless a parent is present. What do you do?

a) Talk to your dad about the party. When he asks if your friend's parents will be there, you say yes. You'll take your chances that he won't find out the truth.

b) Tell your friend, "Thanks, but no thanks." Rules are rules.

c) Tell your mom about the invite, but leave out the fact no parents will be there. If she doesn't ask, you won't tell.

5- You catch your sister texting when she's supposed to be studying—again! You know her grades have been slipping. You decide to:

a) Belt out "BUSTED!" and dash off to tell your parents. Hey, she ratted you out last week, so she has it coming.

b) Offer to keep quiet in exchange for some cash for lunch tomorrow.

c) Roll your eyes, and ask how her homework is going.

6- You're shopping for a school dance. Looking fabulous is a must. Your friend tries on a skirt that she can barely zip and asks if it makes her look chubby. You:

a) Shake your head and say, "Nope! If you like it, you should buy it." But actually, you're not sure it's a good look for her.

b) Look at the skirt closely and say, "I don't know." You don't want to hurt her feelings, but you don't want to encourage her to buy it, either.

c) Say, "It's not very flattering, but if you like it …"

7- The girls are going out for bubble tea tonight. Your mom gave you clearance to go—if your homework is done. Your book report is barely half written. You:

a) Slam the book shut, and declare, "Finished!" Your mom won't know the difference. Besides, you deserve a little fun after spending more than an hour with Huck Finn.

b) Call your friends, and explain the situation. Maybe they can get some tea to-go for you.

c) Beg and plead with your mom. Swear you are so close to being done. You'll finish it when you get home.

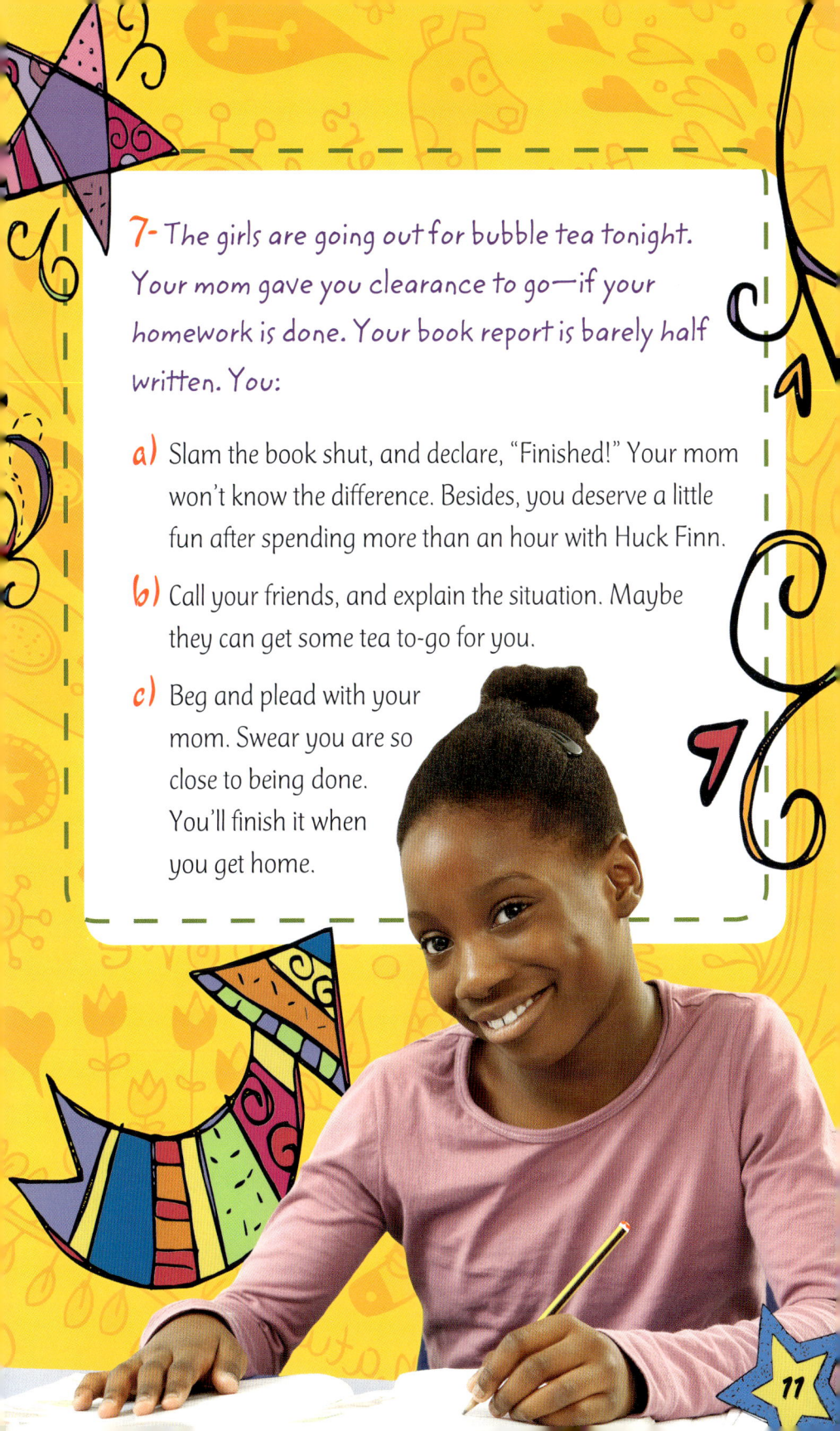

8- A cute guy in your art class is no Picasso, but he tries so hard with every project. His latest mishap looks like he spilled a chicken burrito on his canvas. How do you react?

a) You aren't really sure what is going on with his painting. Is that a hamburger with a mustache? You just smile and nod in appreciation of his effort.

b) You act sincere when you tell him, "You're amazing! I wish I was that creative."

c) Take off your glasses, tilt your head, and squint. Then you shake your head and exclaim: "What is that?"

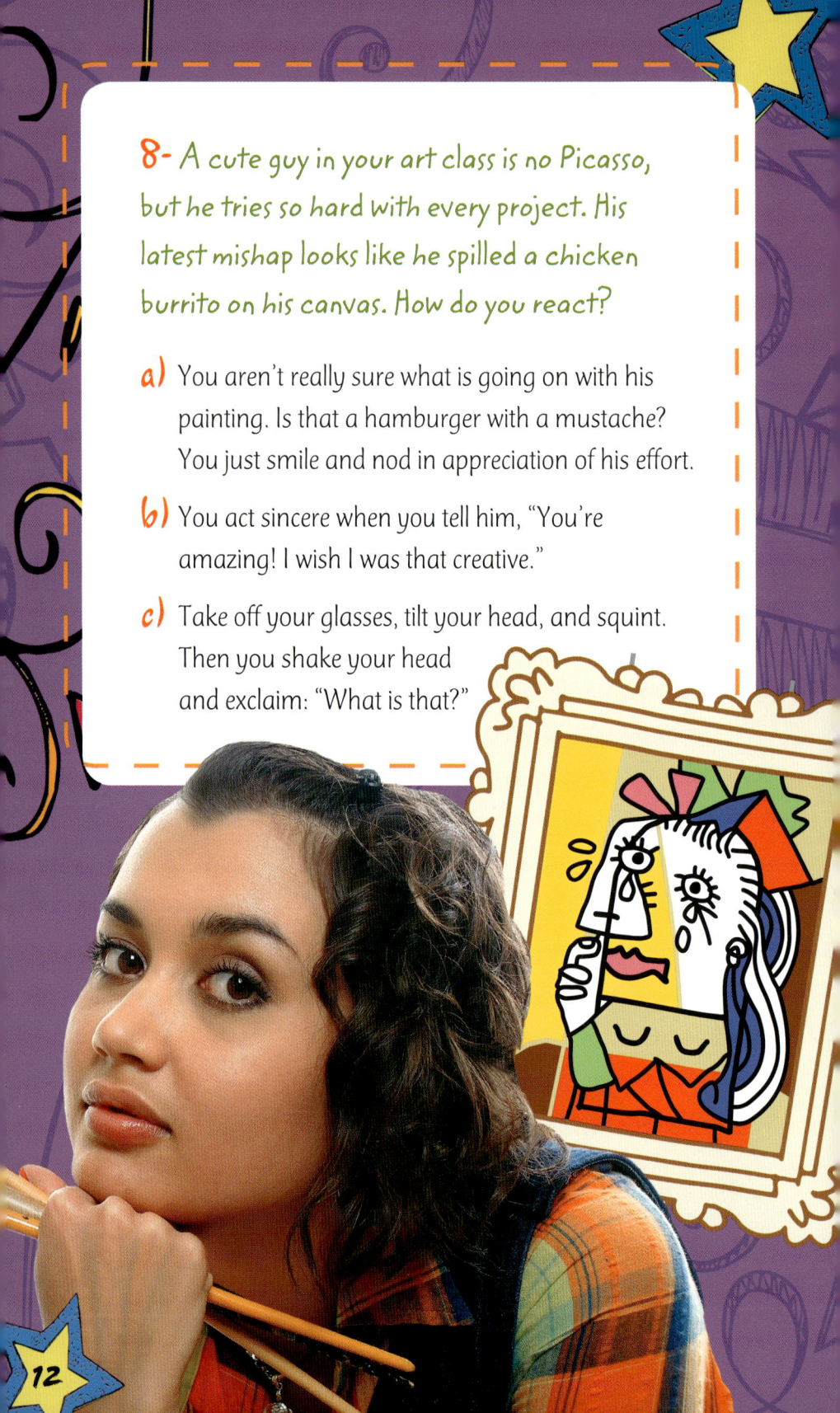

9- One of the guys in your class got the answers to today's history quiz. You didn't read the chapter and can't believe there is going to be a quiz! You:

a) Know cheating is never OK. You let the teacher know the answers were leaked.

b) Pretend you're sick, and spend history class in the school nurse's office.

c) Ask your classmate for a copy of the answers. You'll read the chapter tonight to make up for it.

10- A potential babysitting client asks about your experience caring for babies under a year old. You have ... ummm ... well, no experience. You respond:

a) "Kids that young are uncharted territory for me. But I'm willing to give it a shot."

b) "I work with kids of all ages. Your little munchkin won't be a problem."

c) "The tiny tikes are my specialty!"

11- Panic! Your report on Marie Curie is due today! You thought you had another week to work on it. You quickly come up with a plan to handle the situation. You:

a) Tell your teacher you were going to print it, but your flash drive was missing from your locker. What kind of jerk breaks into lockers?

b) Tell your teacher the truth. Everyone loses track of time once in a while. Maybe she'll give you a deadline extension.

c) Tell your teacher you would really like one more weekend to finish it up. You were so fascinated by the subject that you are way over the word count.

12- Game night with the family is more fun when you win. You're just two spots away from victory! On your roll, the dice tumble off the table. You look and see two threes. You say:

a) "If they fell off the table, I get a roll again, right?"

b) "Ugh! Two threes!"

c) "Yes! I rolled snake eyes—just what I needed!"

13- Your cheer squad's car wash fund-raiser netted twice as much cash as expected! But afterward you are exhausted and hungry. Five bucks could buy you a decent meal:

a) But the money is the squad's, not yours. You bike home and make a sandwich.

b) But if the captain found out, you'd be off the squad for sure. Forget it!

c) And you did more than your share of the work. Next stop—lunch!

14- The Environmental Club is pushing your school to go green. That means some hard-core reducing, reusing, and recycling. As a club member, you try to set an example at school. At home:

a) The trash can is way closer than the recycling bin. You are all about conserving your precious free time.

b) No one in your family cares besides you, so why bother? Forcing them to recycle would needlessly ruffle feathers.

c) It's the same deal. In fact, you set up a new bin and convince your family that recycling cans is worth the extra effort.

15- Your band's bass player missed another practice. You know he's been busy helping out at home since his Army dad deployed. But it has been more than a month since you all played. And your friend could really use the practice. You:

a) Suggest he reconsider his commitment to the band for now. His family should take priority. The band will welcome him back when things slow down.

b) Know he needs some motivation to get him going again. You tell him you heard the drummer suggested kicking him out of the band unless he comes to practice.

c) Tell him the band has no talent without him. His skills are the foundation. A compliment will boost his ego. Hopefully that will inspire him to come to practice more often.

Don't turn the page yet!

It's time to tally your results. Check your answers below. Jot down the number of points you scored for each answer, and then add up your points.

1. a—3; b—1; c—2
2. a—1; b—2; c—3
3. a—3; b—2; c—1
4. a—2; b—1; c—3
5. a—1; b—2; c—3
6. a—2; b—3; c—1
7. a—2; b—1; c—3

8. a—3; b—2; c—1
9. a—1; b—3; c—2
10. a—1; b—2; c—3
11. a—2; b—1; c—3
12. a—3; b—1; c—2
13. a—1; b—3; c—2
14. a—2; b—3; c—1
15. a—1; b—2; c—3

Turn to page 18 if you scored 15 to 25 points.

Turn to page 22 if you scored 26 to 35 points.

Turn to page 26 if you scored 36 to 45 points.

RESULTS

15 to 25 points:

THE TRUTH HURTS, BABY!

You tell the truth, no matter what the consequences are.

The Full Scoop

When it comes to straight talk, you pretty much wrote the book. Your friends know you don't pull any punches—ever. That means they can rely on you to give them the real deal, 24/7. Of course, there are times when a little **discretion** would go a long way. This doesn't mean stretching the truth. It just means using a little **tact**. It takes real skill to gently deliver a potentially painful honest message. And sometimes it's better not to say anything than to be brutally honest.

Real-Life Rx:
Tips You Can Use

•Almost every friend has a topic or two that makes her feel uncomfortable. It might be grades, weight, braces, family, or a billion other things. Try to pinpoint each of your friends' sore spots. Use extra effort to be honest but gentle with them when tackling these touchy subjects.

•Have you hurt someone's feelings by being too **blunt**? First things first. Own up to your mistake. After all, it wasn't your intent to hurt her, right? Let your friend know that you wanted to be honest but expressed it in a less-than-perfect way. Make sure she knows that you are sorry she was hurt.

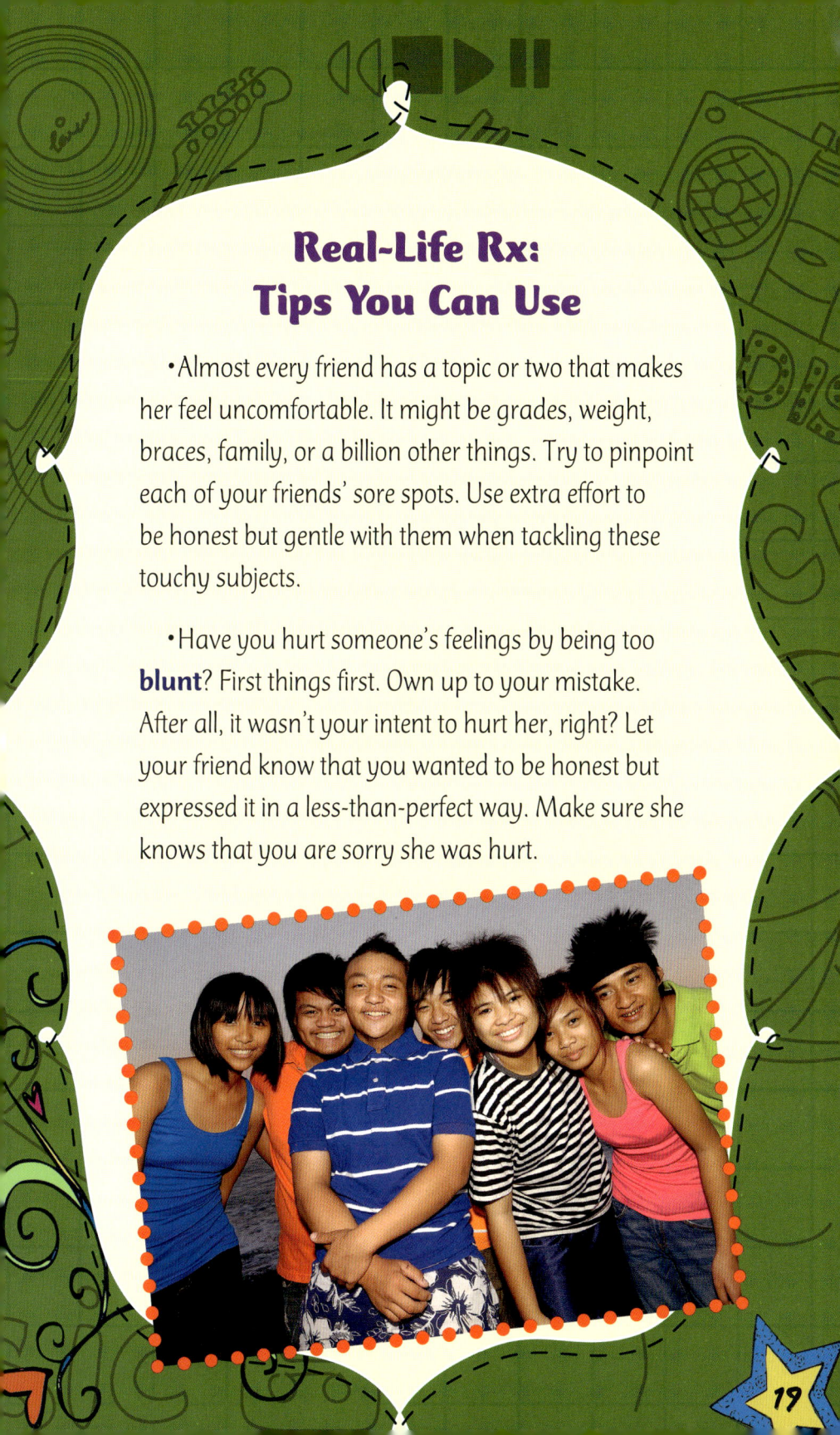

Your Imaginary Alter Ego: Rosalie Hale from Stephenie Meyer's *Twilight* Series

Rosalie was the last of the Cullens' coven to accept Bella as part of the family. Bella treated all the Cullens with respect. Yet Rosalie made no attempt to hide her disapproval for Bella's relationship with Edward, Rosalie's adopted brother. Rosalie says what she feels, no matter what anyone else thinks.

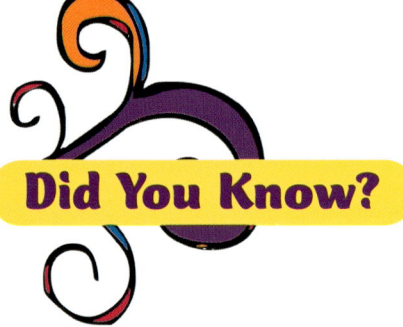

Did You Know?

A machine can sense when someone's lying. It's called a polygraph. The polygraph detects physical changes in a person's body. Things such as heightened pulse, blood pressure, and perspiration indicate stress. Signs of stress suggest the person being tested might be lying. However, not everyone reacts the same while lying, so a polygraph test is not 100 percent accurate.

Researchers believe that body language can reveal when someone is lying. Frequent blinking is one of the most common signs of a fib in action. So are fidgeting and not looking a person in the eye.

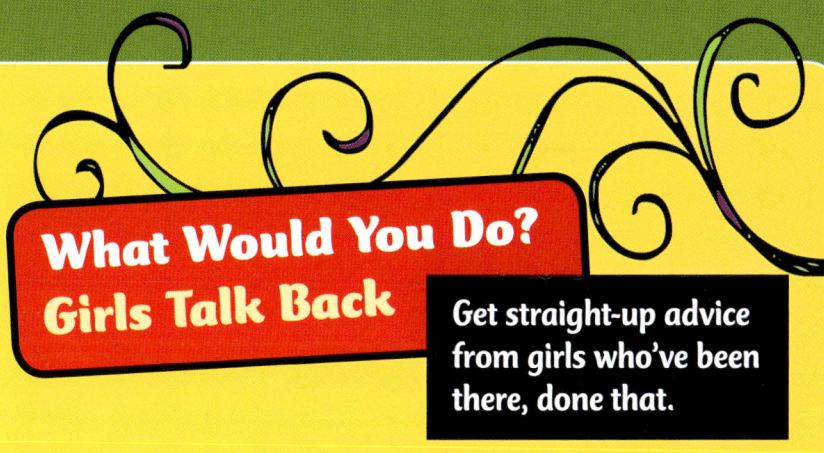

Q: My older sister Bri always seems to be criticizing me. When I get my hair cut, she says it's too short. When I straighten it, she says it looks like a pancake on my head. I like to dress for comfort. She dresses like she walked out of a fashion magazine. And she doesn't hesitate to tell me I look terrible. I love my sister, but sometimes she really makes me feel bad. What should I do?

A: Does Bri know that her comments are hurting your feelings? Be honest with your sis! She might not even know how you feel. She may think she is helping you by pointing out what she thinks is wrong. She might not realize the way she is doing it can be really harsh. Tell her you wouldn't mind having a little help on the fashion front. But that help needs to come in a more positive way. And remind her that she needs to respect your sense of style too. Not everyone wants to be a cover model! A serious dose of honesty on your part may be just what the situation needs.

26 to 35 points:

SMOOTH TALKER

You are often looking out for one person—you! If a small fib or two keeps you out of trouble, you usually think it's worth it.

The Full Scoop

You are pretty good at using words to get what you want—even if that means stretching the truth a little. You have a creative mind and can think on your feet. Both of these are good **traits**. In fact, they have helped you out of many sticky situations, right? But what is the cost? Honesty is an important part of trust and respect. If your friends can't trust you to tell the truth, can they trust you with their secrets or worries? At first glance, it may seem like your actions make life easier for everyone. Take a closer look. Your friendships could be so much deeper and more meaningful if you were more honest. It is priceless to trust your friends with the truth, even if they might not like it.

Real-Life Rx: Tips You Can Use

• Choose one day to tell the truth, the whole truth, and nothing but the truth. No little white lies. Just try it out. You might be refreshed by what you find.

• Lots of lies are simply attempts to ward off awkward or unpleasant situations. But there are always alternatives to telling a lie. Jot down three or four situations where you chose to lie. Now come up with a few different ways you could have handled those same situations.

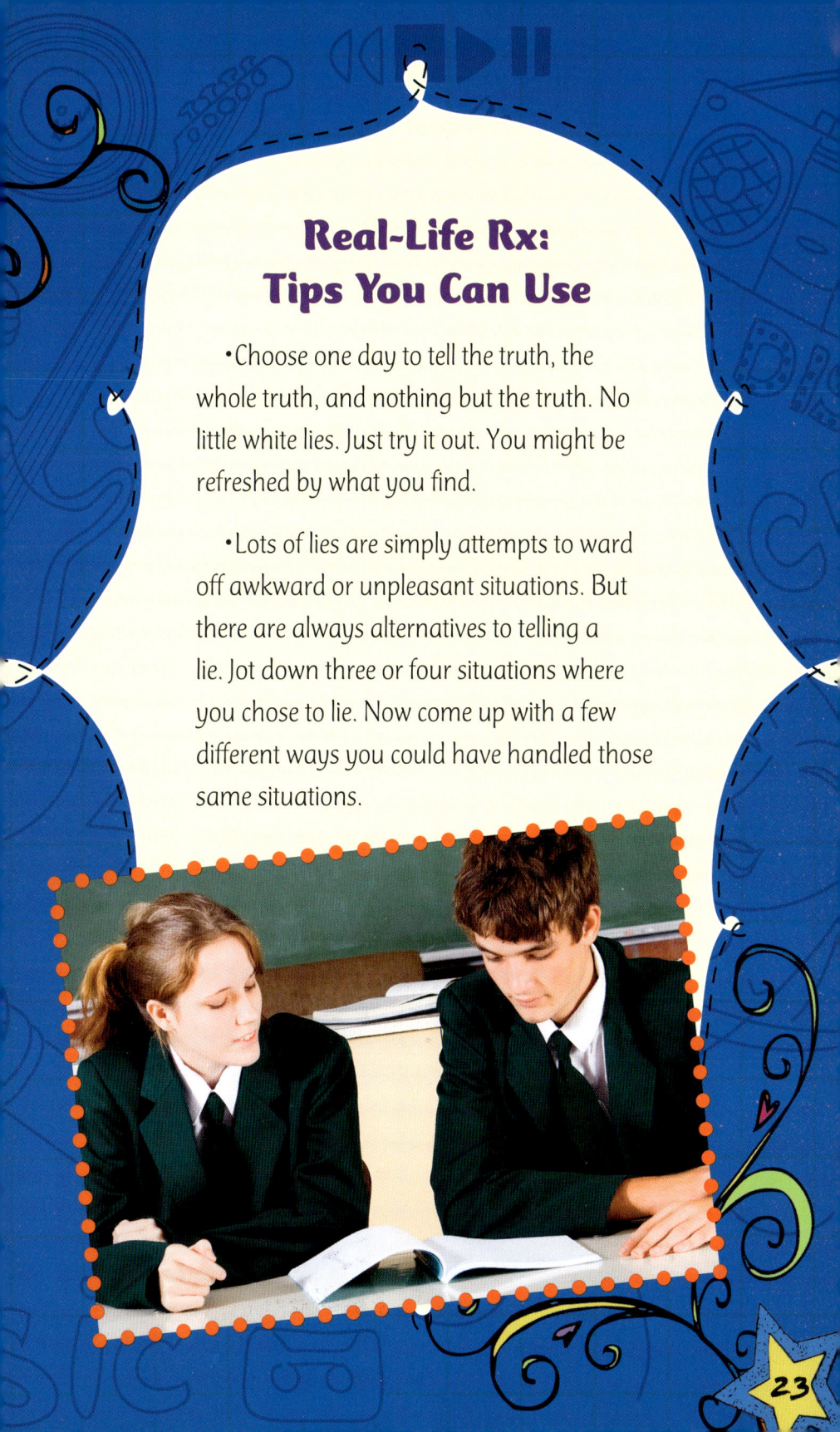

Your Imaginary Alter Ego: London Tipton from *The Suite Life of Zack & Cody* and its spin-off *The Suite Life on Deck*

London Tipton is the only child of a rich business tycoon. She has mad skills when it comes to getting what she wants. London often fudges the facts—whether it's to get a better grade or a date with a cute guy. You might say she depends on her wealth rather than her honesty to enrich her friendships. But despite her attempts to gloss over the truth to get what she wants, London has a good heart. She is loyal to those who matter most to her.

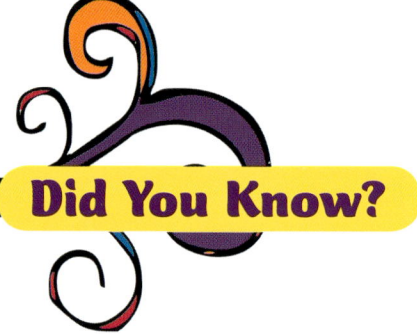

Did You Know?

The Josephson Institute Center for Youth Ethics conducted a survey that included young people's feelings about honesty. It found that 98 percent of students agreed on one thing. "In personal relationships, trust and honesty are essential."

In the same study, more than eight in 10 students confessed they lied to a parent about something significant.

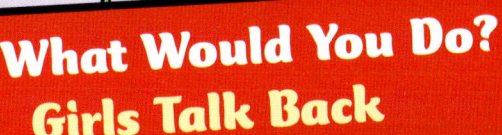

What Would You Do?
Girls Talk Back

Q: For months, my BFF and I have been stashing every cent we can for our class trip to SeaWorld. Then we found a loaded wallet in the mall parking lot. It almost seemed like it was meant for us! It's true that the $250 isn't ours. But maybe this is a reward for being thrifty all year. Is it fair for us to keep the money?

A: OK. Let's think about this for a minute. Finding a padded wallet when you really need the cash might seem like a gift from the vacation gods. But how would you feel if you had lost that wallet? Maybe its owner had been saving up for something special too. When it comes right down to it, the money isn't yours. The best course of action is to turn the wallet in to the police. Maybe the real owner will reward you with money you can feel good about keeping!

36 to 45 points:

THE TRUTH? YOU CAN'T HANDLE THE TRUTH!

All you want is to make your friends happy. But is the cost your own credibility?

The Full Scoop

You value honesty. You really do. But you also value keeping drama to a minimum and pleasing your friends. You are the peacekeeper in your group and don't like ruffling anyone's feathers. Unfortunately, that means that you are sometimes unhappy with your situation. Dealing with **conflict** is not your strength. But guess what? It's something you'll be doing your whole life. Speaking up for yourself and telling the truth take guts. No doubt about it, it's not always easy.

Real-Life Rx: Tips You Can Use

•Many of us want to be perfect—the perfect friend, fashionista, daughter, student, athlete, and on and on. But trying to please everyone can backfire, leaving nothing but a perfect mess. Girl, you need to **prioritize**! Try making a list of all the ways you are trying to be perfect. Then, choose the three roles that are most important to you. Put your whole heart into just these roles for a week, and see what changes.

•You are known for putting everyone else's needs before your own. Why not devote a Saturday afternoon to someone who really deserves a break— you! Take a bubble bath, put your feet up, and pamper yourself!

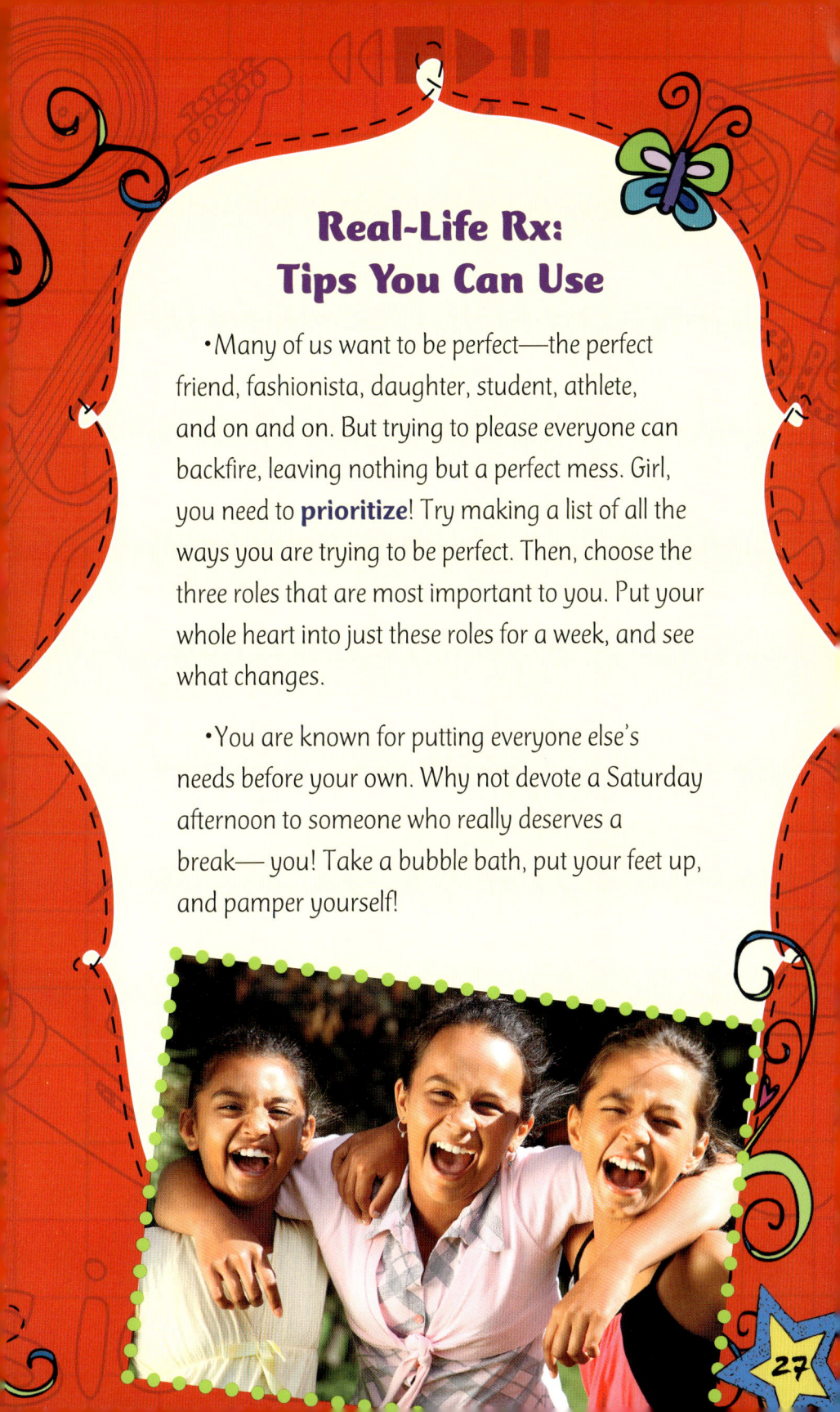

Your Imaginary Alter Ego: Gretchen Weiners from *Mean Girls*

Mean girl Regina is queen of her gorgeous, popular clique, the Plastics. To stay in Regina's good graces, Gretchen will say and do almost anything—from following ridiculous fashion rules to lying about Regina's secret meetings with Shane. Gretchen knows she is being unfair to herself. Yet she chooses to forget the truth to please a bossy friend.

Did You Know?

In a survey in which teens gave adults letter grades in different categories, adults received a C- in "being honest."

Get straight-up advice from girls who've been there, done that.

Q: My childhood friend Shayla isn't very popular at school. She's super shy in class and isn't involved in sports or other school activities. My other, newer friends think Shayla is a loser and that I shouldn't hang out with her. Lately, my friend Hannah says I need to choose between my closest friends and Shayla. If I'm friends with Shayla, I can't stay friends with them. I'm considering lying about my friendship with Shayla so I don't have to give up any of my friends.

A: Sometimes it seems like it would be easier to lie to avoid friendship drama. However, real friends will respect you and your choices. Let Hannah know that you'd never ditch a friend—including her— just because someone told you to. You may want

to look at your relationship with your new friends too. Be honest with yourself. True friends wouldn't make you choose between them and a tried-and-true pal.

Glossary

blunt (BLUHNT)—direct and straightforward in what you say

conflict (KON-flict)—a disagreement

credibility (kred-uh-BIL-uh-tee)—believability

discretion (diss-KRE-shuhn)—ability to choose the right thing to say

prioritize (prye-OR-uh-tyze)—to arrange things in order of importance

tact (TAHKT)—a way of being honest without hurting someone's feelings

trait (TRATE)—a quality or characteristic that makes one person different from another

tutor (TOO-tur)—a teacher who gives lessons to just one student or a small group of students

Read More

Barraclough, Sue. *Honesty.* Exploring Citizenship. Chicago: Heinemann Library, 2010.

Jones, Jen. *How Trustworthy Are You?* Friendship Quizzes. Mankato, Minn.: Capstone Press, 2012.

Pryor, Kimberley Jane. *Honesty.* Values. Tarrytown, N.Y.: Marshall Cavendish Benchmark, 2009.

Internet Sites

FactHound offers a safe, fun way to find Internet sites related to this book. All of the sites on FactHound have been researched by our staff.

Here's all you do:

Visit *www.facthound.com*

Type in this code: 9781429665421

Check out projects, games and lots more at
www.capstonekids.com

Index